How to deal with LYING

Rachel Lynette

PowerKiDS press™
New York

Published in 2009 by The Rosen Publishing Group, Inc.
29 East 21st Street, New York, NY 10010

First Edition

Editor: Joanne Randolph
Book Design: Kate Laczynski
Photo Researcher: Jessica Gerweck

Photo Credits: Cover, pp. 1, 6, 10, 16 Shutterstock.com; p. 4 © Ebby May/Getty Images; p. 8 © Lucille Khornak/Age Fotostock; p. 12 © www.iStockphoto.com/Cliff Parnell; p. 14 © www.iStockphoto.com/Charles Silvey; p. 18 © Simon Watson/Getty Images; p. 20 © Walter Hodges/Getty Images.

Library of Congress Cataloging-in-Publication Data

Lynette, Rachel.
  How to deal with lying / Rachel Lynette. — 1st ed.
      p. cm. — (Let's work it out)
  Includes index.
  ISBN 978-1-4042-4517-4 (library binding)
  1. Truthfulness and falsehood—Juvenile literature. I. Title.
  BJ1421.L96 2009
  177'.3—dc22
                                        2008006985

Manufactured in the United States of America

Contents

Sometimes people lie because they are afraid of getting in trouble. Lying just makes things worse, though.

What Is Lying?

Jamie told his mother that he had done well on his math homework. Jamie's mother was happy. Later, Jamie's mother found the homework in his bag. He had gotten all the problems wrong. Jamie's mother felt sad because Jamie had lied to her. Jamie felt bad, too.

Lying is saying something that you know is not true. Jamie knew that he did not do well on his math homework. When he told his mother that he had done well, he was telling a lie. What could Jamie have done instead?

Jen told her mother her leg hurt because she did not want to go to soccer practice. Her mother made her go anyway, and she ended up having fun!

Why Do People Lie?

People lie for many reasons. A person may lie to keep from getting in trouble. Have you ever lied about breaking or losing something so you would not get in trouble?

Sometimes people lie to make themselves look good. A boy may try to **impress** his friends by telling them that he made a home run when he really struck out.

Sometimes people lie because they do not want to do something. A girl might tell her friend that she already ate her cookies because she does not want to share them.

We may tell lies so we do not hurt other people. Henry acts happy to get this present, even though it is something he already has.

Little Lies

People sometimes tell little lies. A person may lie by **exaggerating**. Exaggerating is bending the truth to make it seem more impressive. Have you ever told your friends that you got an A on a paper when you really only got a B?

A white lie is a lie that is not meant to hurt anyone. Usually, white lies are told to keep from hurting someone's feelings. Cody's grandma made him a sweater. Cody did not like the sweater, but he told his grandma that he did. Cody told a white lie so that he would not hurt his grandma's feelings.

Lying makes people unhappy. This boy's friends will not play with him anymore because he lied to them.

Lying Hurts!

There are two main ways that lying can hurt people. Lying can get you into trouble. Julia wanted to ride her friend's horse, even though she did not know how. She lied to her friend about knowing how to ride. Her friend let her try and she fell off!

Lying can also make people lose their trust in you. When someone lies, other people feel that they cannot trust that person. If you tell lies, people may feel that they cannot count on you to tell the truth. They may not believe you, even when you are telling the truth!

Talking to your friend about why you lied can make you feel better. It can make your friend feel better, too.

When Someone Lies to You

Have you ever had a friend lie to you? You may have felt hurt and **betrayed**. What can you do to make yourself feel better?

First, think about why your friend lied. Was she afraid to tell you something? Second, you may decide to **confront** your friend. Confronting your friend means telling her that you know she lied. When you confront someone about lying, it is important to stay calm. Then tell that person how the lie made you feel. Your friend may explain why she lied and **apologize**. If you can forgive your friend, you will both feel better!

Telling a lie can feel just as bad as being lied to.
Think about why you lied, and then promise
yourself you will not lie again.

What if You Tell a Lie?

When you tell a lie, you may feel afraid of getting caught. You might also feel **guilty** for not telling the truth. Telling a lie does not make you a bad person, but it may mean that you made a bad choice.

The good news is that you can always make a better choice. You can tell the truth! Telling the truth to a person you have lied to can be hard. When you tell the truth, though, you help rebuild trust. Once you have told the truth, you will likely feel better, too!

Lily lied to her best friend, and now her friend does not trust her. How can Lily make things better with her friend?

What if You Get Caught?

Carlos lied to his father about eating all the cookies. He got caught when his father found the bag in his room. Carlos lied again and said his brother put the bag there. What could Carlos have done instead?

It is not fun to be caught in a lie. You may feel **ashamed**. You may feel afraid of getting in trouble or losing a friend. You may want to try to fix the problem by lying again. Lying again will only make things worse. **Admitting** you lied is the first step in making things better.

Telling the truth can be hard, but it is always the right thing to do. These boys know they can trust each other.

Making It Right

After you admit that you told a lie, it is a good idea to apologize. Betraying someone's trust is a **serious** thing. The person you lied to needs to know that you understand that you broke his trust and that you are sorry.

You can apologize for lying even if you do not get caught. People may know that you are lying even if they do not confront you about it. They may not trust you anymore. When you admit you lied and apologize, you help them start to trust you again.

Julie talked to her grandfather about lying to her parents. He said he would support her when she told them the truth.

Put an End to Lying

Once you start lying, it can be hard to stop. One way to keep from lying is to stay away from **situations** in which you might be **tempted** to lie. If you do not do your homework, you might be tempted to lie to your teacher about why it did not get done. If you do your homework, then you will not need to lie.

If you are having trouble with lying, it can be helpful to talk to a trusted adult, such as a teacher, parent, or **counselor**. Talking about your feelings can make it easier to do something hard.

Start Telling the Truth

You can start telling the truth today! Whenever you are tempted to lie, remember how lying can make you feel bad and can hurt other people. Telling the truth can be hard. You may get punished or feel ashamed. In the end, you will feel better about yourself if you do not lie.

If you tell the truth, people will know that you can be trusted. You can feel proud of yourself for being an honest, or truthful, person. You will know that you have the strength to tell the truth, even when it is not easy.

Glossary

admitting (ed-MIT-ing) Saying something is real or true.

apologize (uh-PAH-leh-jyz) To tell someone you are sorry.

ashamed (uh-SHAYMD) Feeling bad because of something you did.

betrayed (bih-TRAYD) Turned against.

confront (kun-FRUNT) To stand up to and disagree with someone.

counselor (KOWN-seh-ler) Someone who talks with people about their feelings and problems and who gives advice.

exaggerating (eg-ZA-juh-rayt-ing) Stretching beyond the truth.

guilty (GIL-tee) Feeling that you have done something wrong.

impress (im-PRES) To make a strong effect on the mind or feelings.

serious (SIR-ee-us) Important.

situations (sih-choo-AY-shunz) Problems or events.

tempted (TEMPT-ed) Felt pulled to do the wrong thing.

Index

Web Sites

Due to the changing nature of Internet links, PowerKids Press has developed an online list of Web sites related to the subject of this book. This site is updated regularly. Please use this link to access the list:

www.powerkidslinks.com/lwio/lying/